An economic truth

Brian Connolly

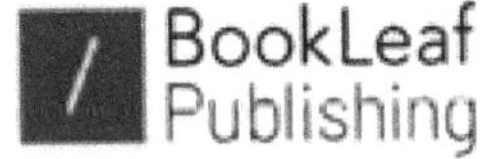
BookLeaf Publishing

Presentation by *BookLeaf Publishing*

Web: www.bookleafpub.com

E-mail: info@bookleafpub.com

ISBN : 9789357210638

First edition 2022

Dedication

Whether professionally or personally, to those who have supported me on my journey, know that I will never be economic in my time with you.

Preface

There is a recognition that the economy is a part of our daily lives. It shapes our behaviours, our beliefs. It holds influence over politics and our pursuit of basic needs. There is a consistent recognition across literature that inequality in society is of growing concern with implications for societal stability and economic progress. There are arguments that existing forms of economic growth and measurement have actively contributed to the inequality currently experienced. This raises the question of: do we serve the economy, or should the economy serve society? To drive forward more progressive economic development, we need to look for how we change the discussion; both through acknowledging current challenges, and then identifying where we can do things differently.

I am due to graduate with a Professional Masters this summer, where I spent the majority of my time exploring the concepts of the wellbeing economy and how the public and private sector could work together in the pursuit of this goal. The majority of my reading over the last 4 years has been dedicated to this topic. Alongside a range of academic articles, I have explored titles such as Doughnut Economics, Economics of Arrival, Trade and Nation, Capitalism and GDP: A brief but affectionate story. I have also sought to understand more about why we grow the economy, with titles such as Poverty Safari, Scotland in a Global Economy, Affluenza and The Scots Crisis of Confidence being great titles to place it within the Scottish context.

This process of undertaking further education also acted as a mechanism to start writing as a means of reflection. I have been using LinkedIn as a means to capture some of my thinking: I sought to understand how the work I delivered was capable of bringing about change. I recognise that initially my writing style was rather basic in form (and content), yet it has evolved as I became more aware of where my reading resonated with my actions. I have been able to create connections between some of the contributors to these discussions. I have sought to consider the output from events and relate it back to where

This collection of poems has come at an interesting time. I am mindful that my learning must be accessible to a wider audience. There is a need to demonstrate competence in a form which helps others identify with the challenges facing the economy, yet recognise where some of these solutions lie. While the initial poems in this collection are very much driven by highlighting concerns (Inequality, GDP), I quickly move on to consider my own experiences in the field of economic development. I have spent time considering areas such as research to facilitate new opportunities. I have provided a number of poems aligned to the key pillars of Community Wealth Building. I have concluded with a poem which looks at things with a more holistic perspective.

These poems are very much my own reflections, yet are based on a changing narrative. In many instances, the poetic subject has informed the form selected, through Acrostic, Haiku, Concrete and many more. I hope these titles help you question the role the economy plays in Scotland and where we can lead change in the world.

The Economic Sea

We establish a journey. The open seas of capital,
consumption and competition.
There is no target set. An assumption of rising
tides which will keep afloat all aspirations.
Yet the only thing that trickles down is the rain.
The economic storm on the horizon.
It is clear to sea, we are no longer in the same
boat.

Some set sail, sold on the stories of success from
those that navigated these waters.
Yet in many ways, these seas were searched and
seized by those with resource.
There was a struggle to plot a course, which
would lead to similar riches.
An attempt to aspire to assets which were
unachievable where economic actors forged
addiction to more.
More material, missing the meaning of what
matters.
We bolstered our buoyancy. Built on the
biographies of our betters.
Yet the waves gathered. The price for progress
was not predicted.

They tower above, taking their toll on those
weighted down by their transactions.
The crash comes to all, yet those who have
tradition on the economic sea are able to travail
the new conditions.
They advise new voyagers that their protections
will be purged, and they should steer directly
into austere waters.
Promises that the tides will change as sure as the
day becomes night; yet the ebb continues on the
shoreline.

There is a desire to narrate a new story in the
grains of sand left behind. Individuals who
remain to shepherd the water that remains.
Forsaking the folly of following in the footsteps
of those who forge tales of fancy.
We have the ability to question who benefits
from continued growth which fails to set a final
destination; only a requirement for limitless
resource.
We must embrace a future which connects us
with our communities and peers overseas, as we
seize the opportunity to address shared
challenges.

No man is an island.

Inequality

What's mine is yours, except when it's not.
Take a few steps back,
don't question the gap.
Born to a home five miles from another.
This delivery dictating the diktat of your daily
drudge.
your education, earnings, employment, and
empathy.
An ability to analyse and acknowledge agitation,
despite apathy from above.

You clamour for crumbs of comfort, as they
trickle down.

A promise that we are all in the same boat,
despite seeing the economic waves crash and
capsize your capacity to remain afloat.
A promise to build back better, relying on a
system forged on crumbling foundations, in the
absence of concrete solutions.
A promise of regeneration, despite your place of
birth becoming a burden to a better life.
A promise of shared prosperity, which fails to
address the generations of missed opportunity.

Whether city, country, or continent,
there is a collapse. A claim on your contribution
centred on conceit.

In equal, what's yours is mine.

GDP

Growth at the heart of everything we do.
Realising there is no end to what we can
achieve.
Only there is a madness to the method.
Sorting data which lacks intelligence as we
clamour for progress which sets us back.
Society left to pick up the pieces of an economy
which counts the rebuild from disaster as
beneficial.

Dominated by a desire to return to normal, we
have lost sight of what normal should be.
Overlooked, the lost generations are challenged
to find hope in a system which looks to their
spend.
Models mastered to measure only our
motivations for more.
Environment, whether ecological or economic
are each embracing exhaustion.
Staring at a statistical fingerprint setup to
stimulate surges in unsustainable sales.
Trends over time, triggered traditions and
trading tournaments.
Indicators of a standard of living which fails to
consider increases in inequalities.

Capturing the costs of our celebration of
consumption.

Progress comes with a high price.
Realising there is a reason to redress the realities
of rampant run-away requisites.
Opportunities to question who does the economy
serve?
Development depends on a desire to drive
destinies.
Understanding the underutilised and their
unrealised capacity.
Capacity to be the capital in their communities
and contribute to real change.
Trade in this measure, aspire to something
better.

Post Growth

We continue to coalesce around the same
conversations about growth,
failing to recognise that tensions continue to
grow.
Debating the value of establishing a destination,
as economists pursue their row.

As individuals we were sold on the promise of
capitalism,
the desire to consume and commit our capital
to the cause of creating a cap.

However, there is no end to this surplus.
We are measured by our capacity to add a plus,
to the financial folly furthered by us.

Whether economic or ecological,
there is now a recognition of the logical
impact of tracking growth by log.

Driven by either incompetence,
or a desire to compete,
we can no longer afford to feed this pet.

We have the intelligence to work with;

Wellbeing establishing a purpose for our planet,
living within the means of it.
Creating a sustainable future for you and I.

To be a Scot

Strong Scots accent of the mind.
Find, attitudes and beliefs, which underpin self.
Wealth measured in deed.
Indeed, there is a person, an individual.
Original, yet struggling to understand.
Withstand; stereotypes stick.
Logic of a world changed.
Shortchanged; our innovation beyond these
shores.
Underscores, our ability to lead.
Succeed in providing solutions.
Contributions which lift us from the floor.
More potential pursued.
Viewed beyond a lack of confidence.
Competence no longer ignored.
Toward a nation with belief.
Relief that our identity is strong.

Purpose

Setting out on a quest to do more.
A passion beyond profit,
a fire which lights the core.
Setting out on a quest to do more.
Thinking not just of the bottom line, but a
chance to explore
the reason for being; the remit.
Setting out on a quest to do more.
A passion beyond profit.

Innovation

Pursuing the paths well-trodden.
Make me doubt the value of
new ways of thinking.
I remind myself
I must rely on the thoughts of others.
Nothing you say will make me believe
in the value of change.
I am sure you can agree
doing what is familiar
is better than
the alternative.

Doesn't bear thinking about.

Doing the same things
because
creating something new
Can only lead to
Failure.

(Please read from bottom)

Researching a Reality

Approaching a new market, yet blind;
Opportunities present themselves yet you
struggle to find
a way forward which is defined.

A desire to innovate, bringing about evolution.
A need for a fresh solution.
Rooted in intelligent contribution.

Your desire leads you to communicate.
Your challenge to those who can create.
An alternative to your current fate.

Articulate your data need.
Transformed through intelligence, with speed.
The creation of knowledge which enables you to
succeed.

The entrepreneur empowered to act.
A decision leads to impact.
The differentiation between fiction and fact.

The Global Scot

Individuals
Driven to deliver more;
A part of Scotland.

A sense of shared pride
Contributing to others
Carving their own path.

The saltire flies high
A shared representation
of vision beyond.

Tartan tempts talent
Transferring their thoughts to those
treasuring triumph.

To procure

Spend a penny, spend a pound;
it raises the question of what we found.
This commitment of capital to commence
change.
Yet what do we get in exchange?
Promises made, as they construct
yet the benefits deduct;
all sense of security,
lost in obscurity.
Instead we must look for a potential contender
to be tender,
as they bid to bring benefit beyond bonus.
The onus
is on the retention of wealth,
avoiding deduction by stealth.
Ensuring our communities benefit
and the company is a good fit;
understanding the local need
before we proceed.

As we address the public spend,
I would recommend
we no longer seek to defend
those who apprehend
our ability to attend

to those whom we intend
to extend a hand.
Instead we should expand
our demands
of firms who seek to stand.
The benefits to a region shall withstand.

The derelict

A building stands with ivied wall.
Rust gathers on the fence, forged to help forget,
the dwellers who defined its previous call,
a form focussed on fulfilment for all,
before it stood only for regret.

Yet broken brick becomes a beacon of benefit.
A chance for the community to commission a
cause.
Finding new value in this abandoned asset,
as they look to commit,
to a new future, the past withdraws.

The passers by, no longer see
a monument to
legacy
but a glimpse of what could be;
a chance to create something new.

Reclaim.
Regenerate.
Reform the name,
of a structure tinged with blame.
This opportunity to identify a sustainable fate.

Investment

Seek out the truth of financial success.
Drive a difference in delivery.
Yet this quest has often failed to progress.
A fear it is destined to misery.

To allow community firms to thrive,
they seek out investment through local means.
Connecting bank and business, fails to drive,
past the stagnation of their broken dreams.

Instead of securing global finance,
there is a means to thrive on local wealth.
Building on what exists, we can advance,
the strength of local economic health.

Through our recirculating capital
There is hope for future collateral.

Fair Work

Fair work for a fair pay,
Yet often this approach has lost its way.
Leaders led astray,
by shareholders holding sway,
over what they,
can and cannot say,
when investment in staff is underway.
There is a clear need to display,
a commitment to employees who stay.
Individuals who seek to repay,
faith in how the business will portray
their approach to work and play.
A recognition that if you survey,
those seeking their next role, they will weigh
up more than empty cliché.
Enter the fray of fair work, the alternative,
risqué.

The inclusive model

Standing as something unique,
A different physique,
As interest reaches its peak.

This body brings a beauty that belongs to an
audience beyond its own,
Something that must be shared, it no longer
stands alone.
Instead looking to be shown.

Often treated as an exception, but a means to
break the rule.
This shape serves as a solution, a fuel
furthering the feelings of fascination, a rare
jewel.

This model is driven by a purpose.
A shining light that takes a form owned by all of
us.
Shaped by those who desire more than what lies
on the surface.

Yet this identity is still sought by the few,
those who seek to pursue
a different view of what we hold to be true.

A community comes together to commit to this
form,
A consortium of consensus centred as they
transform
and employee an attraction to this new norm.

There are many reasons why this openness
appeals,
A reflection on an opportunity that reveals
an inclusive model is one which shares our
ideals.

Unlocking Ambition

Supporting those who seek to do more
A recognition of their potential, their passion,
their purpose
A plan to progress, and pursue their ability
Selected for their desire to deliver and make a
difference as part of their development
Part of a community of champions of change
who consider their contributions
Individuals who identify with the need to invest
in their continuing success
Identifying their impact; illustrating an image of
the ideal ideas
Their learning leads to lessons in leadership
The path to new markets
Qualified questions, in their quest to quantity
quality opportunities
Resilience responding to realities Innovation, the
evolution of their economies
We celebrate their cause as they challenge the
preconceived. They progress.

Everything in its Place

Our places have different needs and
opportunities.
Places centred around people and their plans;
placed to articulate access to assets.
Putting a face to the place.
A place defined by not just the physical.
Yet where projects are placed as part of a larger
vision.
No longer hard to place;
To see where to place fresh investment.
An opportunity which places expertise in the
economy.
A place to reflect on the needs of society.
A purpose which defines the place for
intervention.
Working in partnership, to shape the place at
pace.
A time and a place for everything.
We place our bets, nothing is certain.
Balancing national and local, between a rock
and a hard place.
Yet there is a place for everything and
everything in its place.

This trading nation

Scotland, a nation with sustained sales driven overseas.
Understanding our strengths in sectors which set us apart.
Placing value in our prospective priorities.
Purpose, in both planning and passion for our people.
Opportunities which open our economy.
Responding to new markets which realise our readiness to revolutionise.
Trade, targeted today and tomorrow to transform.
Intelligence helps us identify and inform decisions.
Needs in our companies differ in relation to support.
Global by birth or our sleeping giants, potential performers all.

Economic intervention to help our exporters.
Xenophilia underpins our appreciation of where we can do more.
Proud of our contribution to the world, a nation of innovators.
One Scotland, with clear objectives.

Realistic and resourced.
Time to take our next steps.
Scotland is Now.

The sectoral strength

The revolution is here and will be televised,
technology transformed in tartan.
A digital demonstration of our depth in big data.
To lead rather than follow the financial flows.
Forging new fates for those firms in fintech.
The capacity to cater to companies with contact
centres demonstrating competencies with clients.
Our life led by Science, demonstrating a healthy
commitment to collaboration in the chemical
clusters.
We have our sights set on the skies, satellites and
space set us apart.
The north sea, unwieldy to those who fail to
seek support; our energy to embrace.
We create new futures; narratives nurtured in
new mediums as industry creates.
Renewed and setting out to secure something
sustainable.
Our destinations drive those with a desire to
discover our destiny

Building in the Darkness

Societal disruption
to .
recognise
the essential nature of resilience. We
build.
The public
pursuit of greater.

We face
challenges.
The opportunity of
which will be

a new starting point.

: Inequality,

exposed

the world;

an acute, point of inflection in how we reflect .

The alternative constrained.

We need to
prepare
to match the
future.
We must
transform
in
recovery.

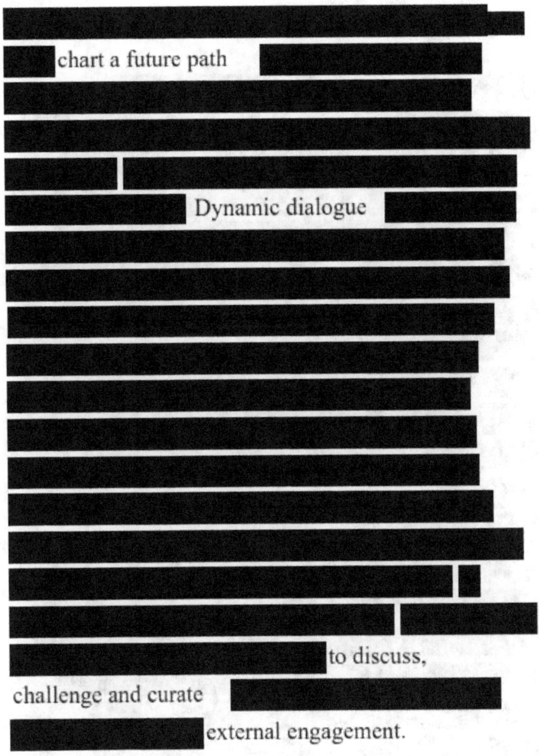

chart a future path
Dynamic dialogue
to discuss,
challenge and curate
external engagement.

Approach
the lens
to take a holistic view.
In doing so, we
understand
progress.

A toast to Scotland

I wander this dear green place, looking for the space to think. To contemplate. The fate of those to come. I was never much one to think to myself, parking those thoughts on the shelve. I head up the high road, trying to justify what I look to do. Yet I can't speak for you. A nation which set the pace. I stop at every passing place. A chance to embrace that which has gone before. Yet the road ahead requires more. Every shore which surrounds the land brings a different message in the sand. Yet washed away.

The saltire flutters in the ever-present wind. A welcome sight, night or day. A sense of being home. Yet a quest to do more. Rooted in a passion which burns bright. The prose which ignites. A Man's a Man for A' That. We look to the soul in the street. What they wear on their feet, dictating what they can eat. A fate, from bairn to burial, built on where you are born. I could walk 5 miles or a hundred more, knocking on the door. Ringing the bell. Knowing fine well, that change can no longer wait.

Well, being from a place, with a well-kempt
face, you may think I can't speak to your woes. I
might look like your foes. Suited and booted.
Yet I look around and I've found a nation that
cares. Aye, a people that wears their hearts on
their sleeves. Who'd roll them up to gie ya a
hand. Who don't care from what land you come.
When you are here, you are a Scot. What we can
do together, will help us weather any cloud, but
the rain which inevitably falls.

I'm no a man of few words, often known for a
haver. Yet I'd ask you a favour. On this day,
when we raise a glass, just pass your thoughts to
your fellow Scot. By blood or bagpipes, we're a'
Jock Tamson's bairns.

www.ingramcontent.com/pod-product-compliance
Lightning Source LLC
Chambersburg PA
CBHW070612160726
48003CB00005B/2242